PEACE OF THE SELF

PEACE OF THE SELF

SANGEETA DEB ROY

Sim's Divinity

CONTENTS

PEACE OF THE SELF

Sangeeta Deb Roy

CHAPTER 2

CHAPTER 3

Table of Contents

CHAPTER 4

AUTHOR'S NOTE

I am a mother, wife, and daughter. While playing these roles, I sometimes tend to hold the weight of the world on my shoulders and fall into despair. I started having stress and anxiety issues myself. My catastrophic thoughts have inhibited me from fully living. Weeks, months, and even years flew by. I became lost in a whirlwind of mental chatter and completely ignored my own being. I wasn't mindful of my feelings or my being. I was always on auto-pilot. I used to feel anxious about anything and everything. Then, to top it all off, I reproached myself for being stressed.

So, I realized it's time I do a considerable life overhaul in order to stop living as a strung-out person. Stress became a cyclical pattern, and I started to fade, but then I embraced the purposeful habits I mentioned in the book. I have been practicing meditation for the last 11 years, and here I am, trying to help others with whatever I have learned in these fateful days. I meditated back when it wasn't the sanctuary as it is now. The payoff is huge and can be life-altering; it certainly has given me my life back!

Peacefulness can be attained when we liberate ourselves from the confines of the mind. The points mentioned in the book are what I have learned to keep myself calm and get me going. These helpful tips that are going to be discussed in this book have transformed my life experiences. That in itself is not a cure-it-all, though, but for me, it brought a shift in my perspective to move ahead in life. I hope this book will be as useful to you as it's for me after embracing these habits.

CHAPTER 5

INTRODUCTION

Stress and unrest of the mind have become such a part of us and our everyday life that we now consider it part of normalcy. So much so that when it starts to infringe on our physical and mental health, we do not even realize it. Many of us are not even aware that our *mind* is constantly thinking. The implications of stress on the mind are highly underrated, even though it is the root cause of many emotional breakdowns and impairments. We also view the art of meditation in the same light as we just described stress. Meditation, however unrecognized, is the answer to numerous stress implications.

In this book, you will learn and discover how meditation can awaken inner peace that leads to happiness and bliss. At the same time, you will realize that you are not the mind, but the consciousness beyond the mind, the boss of your mind.

CHAPTER 6

SECTION ONE

CHAPTER 7

CHAPTER ONE: THE NATURE OF THE MIND

Nature of Mind—The incessant chatter

Our mind is constantly busy, every minute of the day, from the moment we wake up until we fall asleep. Most of these thoughts are meaningless and useless thoughts that pop up in the mind.

The mind also tends to worry, have doubts, and constantly overthink. It often inflates insignificant events beyond proportions, thus creating unnecessary stress and tension.

All kinds of thoughts enter the mind, stay a little while, and then make room for other thoughts. Ideas, thoughts, worries, and fears constantly capture the attention and occupy the mind.

There are also nonstop inner discussions and inner conversations going on.

Your mind can either be your greatest asset or your most dangerous liability, depending on how it is managed. Do you have racing thoughts and find yourself constantly worrying? This is a classic case of an untrained mind. An anxious mind is dreadful.

The problem that underlies all problems is the mind. First of all, it is necessary to know what the mind is, what matter it is made of, and whether it is an entity or just a process, whether it is substantial or just an appearance.

If you don't know the true nature of the mind, you will never be able to solve any of the problems that haunt your life. You can try hard, but you are bound to fail. Mind is the only real problem. So even if you solve this or that problem, it won't do any good because the root will remain intact.

It is just like cutting the branches of a tree so as to prune it without uprooting it. New leaves and new branches will sprout and grow again (i.e., new problems). Your effort will do no good. In that fight, you will waste energy, time, and life, and at the same time, the tree will only grow stronger, thicker and thicker. You will be surprised at what happens: even if you solve a problem with great effort and commitment, the problems will continue to grow and increase. Then, another ten will take the place of the one just solved. Therefore, do not try to deal with individual problems separately: the mind as such is the real problem.

It is hidden underground; it is the root and therefore cannot be seen. When you are faced with a problem, this is in the light of the sun. Hence, you can see it; it is not the root that remains invisible, hidden. So do not struggle with what is manifesting because paradoxically, you will find yourself struggling with shadows, and the same problems will continue to surface.

If you look at your life, you can understand what I mean. I am not speaking of the mind on a theoretical level but of its practical reality.

The mind itself can never be peaceful or silent. By its very nature, it is in tension, in a state of confusion. Clarity, peace, and silence are only possible without the mind. Thus, never try to reach a silent mind because you are moving into an impossible dimension.

So, the first thing to do is to understand the nature of the mind, which is really just a process. In it, there are individual thoughts, which are stirred so quickly that it is impossible to see the intervals between one and the other. And you cannot see these intervals because you are not aware and alert enough: that is, you need a deeper intuition. The moment you can look deeper, suddenly you will spot one thought, then another, and another, but there will be no mind. It is only the set of thoughts, millions of thoughts, that gives you the illusion that the mind exists. It is just like a crowd: as if lots of people are gathered together in a group, which gives you the feeling that there is something you can define as a "crowd." However, in reality, they are just a collection of individuals gathered in the same place. Only individuals exist.

This is the first step in understanding the mind. So watch, and you will find the thoughts, but you will not meet the mind. And if this observation truly becomes your direct experience and an element of your knowledge, suddenly, many things will start to change. You will find that thoughts float and that there are spaces in between. You will then find that the intervals are more numerous than thoughts because each thought must be separate from the other, and each word is separate from the other. The deeper you go, the more intervals you will find, and wider and wider.

If you are unaware, you cannot see these intervals: you jump from one thought to another, never seeing intervals. If, on the other hand, you acquire awareness, you will see more and more spaces; if you become fully aware, then immense spaces will reveal themselves to you. And precisely in those spaces, the Truth will knock on your door. In those spaces, God is realized, or whatever you wish to call this experience.

When awareness is absolute, then there is only a single vast range of nothing. It happens just like with clouds: clouds move, and they can be so dense that you can't see the sky hidden behind them. Then, suddenly, a glimpse into the blue of the infinite sky. The same thing happens inside you; you are the blue vastness of the sky, and thoughts are like clouds that hover over you and fill you.

Therefore, the mind does not exist as a separate entity. Here is the first thing, only thoughts exist. The second thing is that thoughts exist independently of you; they are not one with your nature. However, they come and go; while you continue to exist, you remain. You are like heaven: it is always there. The clouds instead pass, as they are a phenomenon of a few moments; they do not last forever. These thoughts are not yours; they do not belong to you. They are visitors and guests, but they are not the hosts. As long as they stay that way, they are beautiful, but if you completely forget that you are the host and they take your place, then you will be in trouble. They are guests...receive them, take care of them, but do not identify with them; otherwise, they will become your masters. The mind becomes the problem when thoughts are so deeply rooted in you that you completely forget about the distances between you and them.

The morning, the day, the evening, and the night all come, and then they go, but you remain, not as "you." Because this too is a thought, but as pure awareness, therefore, do not identify yourself with your name as this is also a thought. Nor with your body, because one day you will realize that it too is a thought. Just be pure awareness, nameless and formless. Only purity. Since only the real phenomenon of being aware remains. If you identify, you become the mind. If you identify yourself, you become the name, ergo the body. And at this point, what is momentary acquires importance and relevance. What is momentary is the world; the eternal is the divine. This is the second insight you must come to: recognize that you are the master and thoughts are merely guests.

If you keep observing, you will soon come to the third point: you will find that thoughts are foreign, intruding, foreign. No thought belongs to you: they always come in from the outside. You are just a passage. A bird enters the house through a door and flies away from another opening, just like a thought which comes in and out of you. You continue to believe that the thoughts are yours: fight for them, talk, discuss, debate, and try to show that you have thoughts. But no thought is yours, no thought is original, all are borrowed, and they are not even second-hand because they belonged to millions of people before you. A thought is just as external to you as an object.

Thoughts are things, they have strength, but they don't belong to you. They arrive, they dwell within you for a while, then they leave you. The whole universe is filled with thoughts and things: these represent the physical tension of thoughts and the mental tension of things.

This is, therefore, the third intuition: thoughts are things, which have strength, and which must be treated with caution. Usually, however, one continues, unconsciously, to think about anything. It is difficult to find a person who, with the intention, has not, therefore, committed many crimes and all sorts of sins. For example, constantly thinking about killing someone can determine the situation in which that person is killed. Your thought, in fact, can be captured by someone who, being in a condition of weakness, can get to commit that crime.

For this reason, those who have reached the knowledge of the inner essence of man affirm that all of us, in Truth, are responsible for what happens on Earth. There is only one individual who cannot take this responsibility: the one who is in. For the rest, we are all responsible for what happens. If the Earth is hell, we are all its creators.

So do not continue to throw the responsibility on others because it is yours too; it is a phenomenon that affects the whole community. It may be that the "disease" explodes in any place, thousands of miles away from you, but that makes no difference because thought is above space. This is why it travels very fast; not even light travels at the same speed. It doesn't need time to move. Space doesn't exist for it. You can be here, thinking about something, and that thought will bring about an occurrence in a place far away from you, on the other side of the Earth. How can you be held accountable? No court can punish you, but before the supreme court of existence, you will be condemned. Indeed you have already been condemned. That's why you are so unhappy.

Thought is, therefore, even more, insidious than action. Indeed, one can defend oneself from action, but not from thought. Everyone is vulnerable to thinking. Do not think; it is, hence, an indispensable necessity in order to be free from sin, free from crime, free from everything that surrounds us.

So be careful because every thought has some concrete effect. And if you have positive thoughts, you will also have negative ones. Indeed, how can good exist without evil? If you think about love, you will find that hate is hidden right nearby. How do you think about love without not also thinking about hate? Love can reside in the conscious spaces of the mind, but hate can be hidden in the unconscious. Can you think of compassion while not thinking of cruelty? Is it possible to think of non-violence without thinking of violence? The very word "non-violence" contains the word violence; it is included in that same concept.

There is a completely different quality of being which arises from non-thinking: no positive or negative thoughts, simply a state of non-thinking. Just observe, stay aware, but don't think. However, some thoughts will surely enter you because the thoughts are not yours and float in the air. Like air, thought is all around you and continues to enter you on its own. It only stops as your awareness grows, which creates energy stronger than thought.

Awareness is like light. When you turn on a lamp in the house, the darkness is no longer able to enter. However, if you turn it off, the darkness spreads in less than a moment and envelops you. Thoughts are like darkness: they only enter if there is no light inside. So the more aware you become, the fewer thoughts enter you.

If you truly integrate into your awareness, thoughts can no longer enter you: you become like an impregnable citadel. This does not mean being closed; on the contrary, it means being unconditionally open. The energy of awareness itself becomes your stronghold. And if thoughts cannot enter you, they will spin around and go away. You will see them coming, and they will simply take another route.

LEARNING TO SILENCE INCESSANT CHATTER

Learning how to silence the incessant chatter of the mind is such a relief. You have the choice. The realization that you have control over your own life is truly liberating.

- It is the tendency of the mind to think ceaselessly.
- It is the inner monologue that goes on relentlessly in the mind.
- The inner voice constantly analyzes everything about your life, circumstances, and the people you meet.
- It is a voice in the head that just keeps talking and talking!

This inner babble goes on and on in everyone's mind. You might always be aware of this mental noise because it has become a deeply ingrained pattern and is considered a natural and indivisible part of life. If you detect those patterns routinely, you will assuredly know that they impact you in a very real way but also that you can change them.

We all have a voice in our heads that is our constant companion. For most of us, this rumor doesn't mean we are insane. It is a natural part of being human called "thought talk." Often, we are not aware that we are chatting to ourselves, but whether we are aware of it or not, it affects how we feel about ourselves, our lives, our work, and pretty much everything else. It can cheer us up or bring us down unless we learn to monitor and control it. This begins with our understanding that our brains never stop thinking.

The brain has evolved to always be alert. This ensured our survival and allowed us to evolve into the extraordinary beings we are today. All day, all night, our powerful brains process information and make sense of data.

This mental noise is like a background noise that never ceases. Excessive thinking comes from a constant state of fear. Thinking too much is like dreaming during the day. You miss all the joys in life. Imagine and be afraid of what may not happen. Thinking too much is not just a nuisance; it is plaguing.

Excessive thinking causes anxiety, insomnia, paralysis, and depression.

One of the most frustrating things about overthinking is that, more often than not, it feels like it's not going anywhere. No progress is made by all the unwanted efforts that are imposed on you. You simply end up going into the same circles over and over again, resulting only in frustration and misery.

It is time to take charge of our turbulent minds. Taking control of your mind means waking up to the present moment and becoming aware of where you're directing your power of attention. What differentiates happy and unhappy people is often the mental habits they cultivate on a daily basis.

Even in the modern world, our minds are always agitated to find dangers and opportunities in the data we derive from our surroundings, a bit like a search engine server. Our brain takes it one step further, however, even thinking proactively, a task that requires even more mental processing.

Thought chatter is generally harmless and totally random; it jumps from one thought to another for no obvious reason. Some of this seemingly casual chatter helps us make connections to solve problems, create art, make discoveries, and so on. We feel good when it evokes happy memories, the anticipation of future events, the image of our loved ones, and so on, but it also has a dark side. It can turn into a monster that hurls a stream of negativity, self-criticism, and doubt. It can judge our every action and decision and keep us awake at night. It can become a harpy, sinking its claws into us and stealing all joy.

Sometimes we just want to shout, "Shut up," just like someone else was in control of our thoughts.

Our mind is filled with the chaos of swirling thoughts over which we have little or no control. We feel unstable and uncomfortable, the same way we feel when there is a strong disturbance outside of us.

Though thought chatter may seem out of our control, we have the power to turn it off on demand. The challenge is to notice when it has plunged us into darkness. We do this by monitoring our moods. Like the chatter of thought, our moods range from positive to negative and can change in an instant. We are elated because we are on vacation in Greece; we are immediately discouraged when our flight is canceled. Our moods go up and down like a perpetual motion yo-yo, which makes them the perfect tools to notice that negative thought chatter has taken over. So, how does it work?

The former could not stop considering carefully whether the saber-toothed tiger lurking in the bushes was safe or not. Our brains do the same kind of instant assessments today. Our mood then corresponds to our thoughts about something. When we think it is good, our mood is positive and vice versa. Hence, if we monitor our mood, we can go back to the thought chatter that created it. If our mood is high, the small talk focuses on thoughts that generate positive emotions and vice versa. Once we are aware of this, we can nurture our positive, chatty thoughts to keep our mood high, and we can stop negative chatter to improve our mood.

What's your mood right now? Is it up or down? If so, keep thinking about those happy thoughts. If it's inactive, here are five actions you can take to stop negative chatter and feel better.

1. Embrace Distractions

While distractions are bad for productivity, they provide quick relief from a bad mood. Shelley H. Carson, a psychology researcher, suggests a simple way to distract the chatter of thought: focus on physical sensations and the surrounding environment. Notice how the light bounces off the surfaces. Touch everything on your desk, pick it up, turn it over, and pay attention to every detail as if you've never seen it before. Feel your feet on the floor, your sitting on the chair, the temperature in the room, the flow of air. After a few minutes of this focused activity, notice your mood. It has probably improved. Sometimes, you won't be able to remember which thoughts triggered it, which is good. You don't want to summon them again.

Distraction works because it disrupts your mood and forces you to 'shift gears.' Many negative moods contain an element of reflection about them. When you ruminate, you rethink your problem or worry again and again in your mind. Whenever you look into your problem or concern, you strengthen its grip on you. Distraction breaks this hold by forcing you to think about other things. If the thing you distract yourself with is convincing enough or requires your attention, you will temporarily stop ruminating, and you will start to feel better.

Turn on the television; immerse yourself in a book or video game; play chess, word games, or Sudoku with your phone. Do something that catches and holds your attention and quiet chatter.

2. Breathe the Chatter Until Silence

When you recognize that your mood is low, start breathing slowly and deliberately. Focus on the sensation of the air as you inhale, notice the slight pause at the beginning of the inhalation, then sigh as you exhale and note the slight pause before the next inhalation. Once you are in the groove, start counting each inhale and exhale. You may find that the chatter gets louder and more insistent before it starts to fade. I automatically turn to a breathing meditation when the chatter of negative thoughts becomes unruly and threatens my peace of mind. I close my eyes, keep my hands on my face, and breathe as if there is no other activity in the world.

3. Starve the Monster

Negative moods are the product of negative thinking about something. As the emotional response to negative thought chatter increases, the neurotransmitters associated with stress are released.

Adrenaline is the fight or flight hormone and fuels your immediate reaction. Even if a saber-toothed tiger isn't jumping at you, your body behaves like it is.

Norepinephrine is similar to adrenaline and increases the excitement of adrenaline. Now, you have a double dose flowing through your system. Unsurprisingly, your hands start shaking, and you want to escape.

Cortisol is the stress hormone. It comes later but serves to keep the excitement alive by releasing a new soup of different chemicals.

Stop feeding thoughts!

According to Dr. Jill Bolte Taylor, a neuroanatomist, in her book *My Stroke of Insight: A Brain Scientist's Personal Journey*, neurochemicals leave your body in 90 seconds as long as you stop the thought chatter that is triggering them. Set a 90-second timer and consciously breathe or distract until the timer goes off. If you are diligent, at the end of 90 seconds, the chemical soup is gone, and so are the symptoms of stress.

4. Awareness

Be aware of what's going on in your head. It sounds simple. Are you thinking too much? Are you thinking negatively? Admit it. Because otherwise, you won't change anything. Self-improvement begins with self-acceptance. Once you are aware of what needs to be corrected to help yourself, you can make a real change.

By keeping a thought journal, you will have in writing what is going on in your mind, and it will be much easier to make the changes you want to make as you will know what is really happening.

5. Intrusive thoughts

An intrusive thought is an involuntary thought, an un-wanted, unpleasant image or idea that can become an obsession, is upsetting or distressing and can seem difficult to manage or eliminate.

When intrusive thoughts invade the brain, they create neural pathways that get stronger over time. You can't control how these thoughts come in; they are intrusive. But you can control how you respond to them.

- Don't fight them.
- Don't try to put them away.
- Don't try to argue against them.
- If you do, you will make them stronger.

Instead, it is better to practice non-resistance. Observe your thoughts instead of holding on to your thoughts or rejecting them.

The practice of observing your thoughts in a detached way is called mindfulness meditation. (We'll talk a little more on this in a later chapter).

6. Control the chatter with meditation

Meditation is an extremely important, unique mechanism for putting inner dialogue under control. Mediation is the most effective technique that can calm the monkey mind. As you meditate, you train your mind to stop the inner dialogue, restore your strength and bring your thoughts under control. If you meditate every day, you have less difficulty in silencing the monkey. The practice of this meditation is perfectly suited to the neuroacoustic programs of the Institute of Development of Consciousness. Research into the benefits of meditation is full of its calming effects and its ability to calm the chatter of thought. People unfamiliar with meditation often picture a yogi sitting cross-legged on a mat and immediately decide that he is not for them. But meditation comes with a wide variety of options that don't require agility, mats, or anything other than your attention.

Although you may learn a specific meditation practice, all you need to do is focus on what you are doing while doing it because Mindfulness is a form of meditation. The goal is to become present and avoid following your talk of thought. A regular meditation practice can be nothing more than sitting silently in your favorite chair and focusing your attention on one thing: your breath, the sounds you hear, or a meditation object such as a worry stone or beads. You can do this while washing the dishes, raking leaves, sweeping the floor, boarding the train, or making dinner.

Don't expect stellar results right away, and don't be discouraged if your thoughts take you away. One minute you are focused on your breath, on a mantra, or on the potato you are tearing, and the next, you realize you have lost five minutes in thought chatter. Most meditators, even long-term ones, admit that their thoughts distract them while meditating. The solution is not to follow them; instead, refocus your attention on your practice.

CHAPTER TWO: WHAT IS STRESS?

As a mother, a father, a husband, a wife, a worker, and a business owner, stress is commonplace and unavoidable. Stress means that the carrying load is greater than the carrying capacity. You have the feeling that you cannot meet the demands that are made of you, and because of this, you feel tension and pressure. A certain amount of stress is necessary to function properly. Stress causes your body to move—your heart beats faster, and your breathing accelerates so that oxygen comes in. But it also strengthens your focus and puts your body (and mind) 'on edge.' Hence, it ensures that you can do things, but it should not be too intense or last too long. Then, it is also called unhealthy stress.

Situations in which you can experience a little 'healthy' stress are, for example, if you still have mountains of work to do and the deadline is getting closer. Or, you experience holiday stress because you leave for the sun tomorrow and the suitcases are not yet packed. Or, if there is a visitor on the doorstep in an hour and you still have to start cleaning the house. Though, there are many situations in which you can experience 'unhealthy' stress, such as persistent pressure from work or school, stress due to financial problems, or the death of a loved one.

It is a fact that without a certain amount of stress, we, as humans, would be less productive and also less creative. Also, without stress, our performance level would be lower; many people perform better under a certain pressure. However, this pressure should not be too high or occur too often. Being under constant stress inevitably leads to psychological and physical complaints. What is experienced as a stressful situation differs from person to person. In order to function pleasantly and productively and not get sick, there must be a balance between the amount of stress that you experience and can handle (this is individual and personal!) and the amount that you—whether or not forced—to take on. The bow cannot always be tense!

Stress can be distinguished between acute and chronic stress. Also called healthy or unhealthy stress. It is normal to get tense in certain situations, such as during an important presentation or during a (driving) test. We also call this acute stress, and this ensures that you are 'on alert.' Acute stress ensures that you function as well as possible in an emergency situation, such as danger or intense exertion. Your blood pressure and heart rate rise, your breathing speeds up, and your body produces adrenaline. When the 'danger' is over, or you have completed the task, your body settles down again, and you have to recover. After the situation, the balance between the carrying capacity and the carrying capacity is restored. This relaxation ensures that the effects of stress subside so that you can handle a new situation well.

However, there are also situations in which you are under prolonged stress, such as stress due to your relationship or a divorce, trauma, loss, a high workload, or study stress. If you continuously have the feeling that you are under tension or that you have to 'fight' or 'flight,' we speak of chronic stress. Even if you do not get out of a state of stress when the danger has passed, there is a risk of chronic stress. If this is the case, then there is no balance between exertion and relaxation, and your body is not recovering. This is unhealthy stress.

If you continuously have the feeling that you are under tension or that you have to 'fight' or 'flight,' we speak of chronic stress. Even if you do not get out of a state of stress when the danger has passed, there is a risk of chronic stress.

Chronic stress negatively affects how you feel. Your muscles are constantly tense, you are tired, you find it difficult to concentrate, or you suffer from a lot of (tension) headaches. Chronic stress increases the risk of overstimulation, heart rhythm disorders, and other psychological complaints such as burnout, anxiety disorder, and depression.

SYMPTOMS OF STRESS

The symptoms you experience when you are under stress are called stress reactions. Some experience certain symptoms more than others. It is important that you recognize the signs of stress.

Now, how do you know if your stress level is enough to worry about? Here are some symptoms.

Stress symptoms are on four levels:

1. Physical Stress Symptoms

Stress causes physical reactions. Physical complaints that regularly occur during stress are:

- Headache
- Nausea
- Stomach upset
- Tense muscles in, for example, your neck, jaws, or shoulders
- Dizzy spells
- Excessive sweating
- Accelerated heart rate and/or breathing
- Vibrate
- Raised blood pressure
- (chronic) Hyperventilation
- Skin conditions
- Sleeping problems
- Fatigue

Chronic stress makes you exhausted, which can make you feel tired. Sufficient sleep is therefore important, but this is difficult if you have sleeping problems due to stress.

CHAPTER 9

2. Emotional and Cognitive Stress Symptoms

Under the influence of stress, certain emotions are more prevalent, such as frustration, anger, irritability, and fear. This is due to the stress hormones that are released during stress. These hormones have an inhibitory effect on certain areas in the brain. Anxiety is a natural stress response, but chronic stress also makes you feel constantly anxious for no apparent reason.

Mental processes, including information processing and emotion regulation, are also disrupted by stress. In the cognitive field, you can recognize these complaints:

- Obsessive thoughts
- Memory problems
- Concentration problems and worry

3. Stress Symptoms in Behavior

You may also experience stress symptoms at a behavioral level. At the behavioral level, the following stress reactions occur:

- Avoidance

- Aggression
- Eating too much/too little
- Being overly active
- Doing too much at once
- Smoke more
- Drink more alcohol or coffee
- Being chaotic and losing the overview

When using addictive substances, your body always makes dopamine, which creates a feeling of pleasure, and you do not feel the stress for a while. It is therefore tempting to smoke (more) or to flee into alcohol or drugs, and so you can develop an addiction or other problems. Physically, this actually only backfires and creates more stress.

4. Stress Symptoms in a Social Environment

If you experience stress, you can also notice this in the interaction with your environment. For example, stress can lead to reduced interest in the environment and conflicts at home or at work. This is because you are more irritable and experience more negative thoughts and emotions.

WHAT ARE THE CAUSES OF STRESS?

There are various causes of stress. The most common causes are illness or death of a loved one and high work pressure. They are called causes of stress or stressors. We divide these into two different categories: psychological stressors and physiological stressors.

Psychological and Physiological Causes of Stress

Psychological stressors are situations, comments, persons, or events that you perceive as negative or threatening where you have the idea that the environment asks more of you than you can actually handle. Examples include divorce, deadlines at work, and study pressure. Physiological stressors are especially taxing on your body. Some examples include pain, illness, and injuries.

This can get you into a vicious circle. Because the stress affects your immune system, you can literally get sick. This can cause stomach pain or headaches, for example. These complaints cause more stress and thus reinforce each other.

EXAMPLES OF CAUSES OF STRESS

Stress has many different causes. You may recognize yourself in one of these examples.

Work stress

1 in 7 employees experiences work stress. They experience stress in their work situation and often because of a high workload. If you recognize yourself in this, there is a good chance that your workload is also too high and is too much of a burden for you. This often makes you function worse at work, and that can also cause stress. You're going to run after the facts. Always take work stress seriously because it can be a sign that you are taking too much on your fork and eventually lead to absenteeism or illness.

Study

Students are also increasingly experiencing stress. More and more students are experiencing burnout because they experience a lot of pressure during their student days.

Stress after the Death of a Loved One

Losing a loved one is an extremely heavy grieving process, which is accompanied by a lot of emotions. This process demands a lot from you and often causes a lot of stress. In addition, after the death of a loved one, you can also sleep less well; you find it harder to concentrate, and sometimes things simply pass you by. This can also lead to possible frustration and stress.

Stress in (Chronic) Physical Illness

If you are dealing with a (chronic) illness, this can lead to a lot of uncertainty. You do not always know immediately what will happen and how the disease will develop. That can also be very stressful for people.

Stress due to relationship

A good relationship does not happen by itself. You have to do something about that. In one period, it is very easy, and in another period, it is hard work. Relationship problems can certainly also cause stress.

Stress with financial problems

Money problems can cause a lot of stress. You may lie awake at night, experience anxiety, or it affects your self-confidence or social circle. As a result, having debts can even be the cause of psychological complaints, especially if you don't know (yet) how you're going to get out of financial problems.

SENSITIVITY TO STRESS

Everyone experiences stress differently. Perhaps you quickly experience (too much) stress, or you are less likely to suffer from it. The way you experience stress depends on a number of factors:

Characteristics

If you have a positive attitude, you are often less sensitive to stress than if you are pessimistic. On the other hand, qualities such as high sensitivity, difficulty setting boundaries, loyalty, low self-esteem, fear of failure, and ambition make you more sensitive to stress.

Other qualities that pose a risk for stress are perfectionism, performance orientation, competitive pressure, poor planning, and a great sense of responsibility.

CHAPTER 10

Your environment

If you are exposed to severe stress in your youth (the first four years of life), this makes you more sensitive to stressors later in life. These can be, for example, traumatic experiences and an unstable environment.

For example, if you have a good social life and can vent everything during a conversation with your partner after a long day, this lowers the risk of stress. Social support appears to be a good 'buffer.'

Genetic

A mother with a high-stress sensitivity can pass this on to her child in the first eight weeks of pregnancy. Her own high levels of cortisol (a stress hormone) can ensure that she gives the child a lifelong above-average stress sensitivity of the brain. As a result, once outside the abdomen, the brain can react strongly to mild stressors (also in adulthood).

Degree of control

The degree of need for control also partly determines when you experience stress. If you like to be in control, you find yourself in a situation based on fear. You are afraid of letting go of things and of the unknown. Because you try to get away from things with this, this can cause extra stress.

PSYCHOLOGICAL IMPLICATIONS OF STRESS

Stress can cause psychological and mental consequences. Such alterations include impaired executive function, processing speed, and memory and attention. The physical and mental alterations that occur as consequences of stress are:

- Anxiety disorders
- Generalized anxiety
- Panic attack
- Phobia
- Obsessive and compulsive disorder
- Mood disorders

Below is a brief description of each of these disorders.

CHAPTER 11

Anxiety Disorders

Anxiety and stress are two different types of ailments. They are mistakenly confused as if they were the same disease. However, stress may cause an anxiety reaction.

This is how, in the face of some stress trigger, the person suffers an unpleasant emotion. On the other hand, it should be considered that anxiety is an alert reaction. This means that it is not negative in essence. Now, if anxiety occurs excessively, it can cause severe problems.

Hence, the anxiety produced by stress affects behavior. It also alters the psychophysiological state of the person.

Generalized Anxiety

This type of disturbance is equivalent to chronic anxiety. Stress can cause intense symptoms of anxiety; it is identified as a consequence of stress when it cannot be controlled.

It is also determined as an alteration due to stress when a real cause that causes the symptoms of anxiety is not identified.

Panic attack

This type of psychological or mental alteration occurs as an intense fear that appears suddenly. A panic attack includes the feeling of loss of control. Some of the symptoms of panic attacks due to stress are chest pain, dizziness, and tremor, among others.

Phobia

Phobia occurs as a result of stress. It is usually accompanied by intense and distressing panic.

Phobias are not always alterations produced by stress. However, they can be triggered due to stressful circumstances.

Obsessive-Compulsive Disorder

This type of disorder, as a stress disorder, manifests as intrusive thoughts or ideas. The person suffering from stress cannot control such ideas or thoughts. This is how repetitive or ritual behaviors originate as an attempt to neutralize the anguish caused by stress.

Mood Disorders

These psychological or mental alterations occur with episodes of prolonged stress. This is how sensations such as:

- Depression
- Guilt
- Restlessness
- hopelessness
- Irritability.

Stress can create a vicious and endless cycle. This occurs because of depression; this, at the same time, increases stress levels. Similarly, stress can cause other types of disorders such as:

- Eating Disorders
- Bipolar Disorder

- Harmful behaviors, among others.

All these alterations should lead us to remain alert to manifestations of stress. In case of suffering any of the psychological alterations, seek professional help.

To avoid psychological disturbances, it is best to have professional guidance. A traditional psychologist can provide therapeutic treatment to prevent or control stress.

SECTION TWO

CHAPTER THREE:GAINING CONTROL OF YOUR MIND

Feeling out of control or not in control of an important part of one's life is undoubtedly a source of discomfort. It is therefore not surprising that people who suffer from stress, anxiety, tension, and psychosomatic illnesses are also those who allow themselves to be dominated most by external influences. In mind control, there is the fact that we must be clear about: there is no magic in this type of process, but there is a lot of psychology. We are facing that valuable ability that we should all train at some point, to manage our inner world in an intelligent, constructive, and useful way.

It is often said that people have a real obsession with controlling everything, even ourselves. However, it is an impossible goal to achieve in its entirety (which does not mean that we do not have room for improvement).

Mental control can help us, among other things, and reduce the impact of stress. Far from seeing this competition as an almost supernatural ability, we must understand it as that ability that, put in our favor, can mediate balance and well-being. After all, controlling your thoughts is key to improving your mood, your focus, and even your productivity.

Our mental universe is very similar to that of a computer. We create connections, thoughts travel through electrical impulses, and we also have a highly specialized brain. However, there is something that clearly differentiates us from machines: our emotions and our sense of conscience.

A good number of people would not know how to identify their deepest motivations or expose those internal realities by which they start, maintain or end their behaviors/habits.

In this way, a key strategy to increase our mental control (and well-being) is to delve into ourselves. Knowing who we are, what identifies us, and what we expect allows us to find the motivation to take charge of our lives.

We go from one thought to another and from one behavior to another without having the slightest idea why. We feel that it is life that "is taking us," although we do not know exactly where.

It would be impossible to be aware of everything all the time: we would practically have to give up our mental life. We would collapse. What is possible is to pause and stop along the way to contemplate where we are and if we are on the path that we really want to travel. Those pauses translate into greater awareness and this, in turn, into more mind control. Slow down, appreciate the present, and take control.

Learning to deactivate the impulse of an emotion is not easy, especially if we were raised in an environment that didn't place great importance on impulse control. Perhaps our current lifestyle is ruled by haste, demand, anxiety, and "I have to have everything ready for tomorrow." Learning to be more present, slow down and manage our emotions is a big step forward. One way to train our mental focus to appreciate the here and now and increase mental control is through the practice of Mindfulness. Studies show us that this discipline is very beneficial for reducing the impact of anxiety and mediating our psychological well-being.

It is also important to learn to chew and digest frustration. Who has not experienced frustration (that feeling that reality does not conform to our expectations, that which appears when despite all our efforts, we do not obtain the desired result)? Some in small doses, and some giant. A love that was not, a vocation that did not see the light, money that is needed. The reasons can be many. We are all immersed in a reality that forces us to constantly give up. It is normal. The point is that some people accept it and others don't.

It is not easy to learn to accept, chew and digest frustration. If we don't, it's easy for anger to take over our hearts and come to dominate our minds and our lives. It is also easy for us to become curmudgeons (which is not worth it). Let us, therefore, learn to manage these discomforts to improve our emotional health.

Leaving the comfort zone brings immense benefits. One of the most important benefits is that it helps us to be more flexible and adaptable. This, in turn, stimulates the development of our intelligence, both logical and emotional. So finally, almost without realizing it, as if it were a side effect of our attitude, we become more tolerant and masters of our own emotions.

We are not machines, and we do not have to "function" correctly all the time. The topic of mind control should always be taken relatively, especially when it puts a lot of pressure on us.

Strengthen your emotional intelligence. Emotional intelligence refers to the ability of people to recognize their own emotions and those of others and encompasses the development of empathy and social skills. You can also try to set realistic goals. It will help you stay focused on the goal and promote your mental health. The mastery of our emotions increases when anxiety decreases.

Therefore, let us apply these psychological tools on a daily basis to improve the quality and control of our thoughts.

CHAPTER FOUR: THE STEPS TO GAINING CONTROL OF YOUR MIND

What would happen instead if you took active control of your mind and focused on making your life a masterpiece?

What would it be like if you committed to reprogramming your mind and your way of thinking to create a life capable of giving you satisfaction, joy, and passion?

Reprogramming your mind is the key to your success! If you want to live the life you want, then now is the time to decide, commit and take action. The first step is to be absolutely clear about what you want in life. Clarity represents your potential; the more precise you are, the more grounded your vision will be, and the more your brain will seek the tools and ways to transform your vision into reality. It's time to decide what you want now and in the future and how to reprogram your mind. What do you want to achieve physically, financially, emotionally, spiritually, in business, and in your personal life? Make a decision that you no longer want to live the way you are living and focus on the results you want to achieve.

Remember that you are never 100% in control of the situation. Think about this: is your life going exactly like the plan you made in your mind? Probably not.

Life is never a straight line, which is why it is of fundamental importance to remain flexible along the way: learn from mistakes, accept failures, and use negativity as a force to make changes. By reprogramming your mind and changing your approach, you will achieve results regardless of the obstacles and difficulties you encounter in your path.

That sense of frustration will become a gift because it will mean that you are in the moment of the turning point, failure will be a lesson to do better in the future, and any emotional, physical or mental difficulty will become an opportunity to find new and creative solutions.

Here are the three powerful ways to disempower intrusive thoughts and actions that will help you be in control of your mind. They are:

- Mindful meditation
- Let go
- Gratitude

CHAPTER 15

CHAPTER FIVE:MINDFULNESS MEDITATION

A way to get in touch with the depth of the present moment, with what happens inside and outside of us. This is Mindfulness (awareness meditation), in fact, a method to take care of the body and mind, manage illness, stress, and pain, and thus be able to effectively face the challenges of daily life.

Being aware might seem like a trivial concept were it not for the fact that almost always, in reality, our mind is elsewhere. The superstructures of society, together with the way in which we have been raised and the rhythms that are imposed on us, have led us to be constantly in the balance between memories and regrets (past) and anxiety (future). It almost seems that there is no room for the present moment. You become aware every time you bring awareness to the present moment and to what characterizes it.

Scientific research has shown time and time again in recent years that when we train the brain to be in the "here and now," we are actually reshaping its physical structure.

Awareness is not something mysterious or esoteric. It is familiar to us precisely because it is something that is already part of us, even if it takes many forms and presents itself under many names.

We all have the ability to be present, and practicing Mindfulness absolutely does not require us to change who we are.

Mindfulness offers intensive training in mindfulness meditation (better known as calm and insight), also defined as "intentional self-regulation of attention." The ultimate goal of mindfulness meditation is to reduce the level of stress and lead to a deep and liberating acceptance of the disease or situation of profound distress.

WHAT IS MINDFULNESS MEDITATION?

Mindfulness meditation is a practice based on awareness of the moment and on the importance of attention at any moment of the day. When we are truly attentive, we can listen, understand and analyze the external and internal situations of our minds in a neutral way. This act allows us to live reality in a more serene way and stems inner suffering until we reach a complete acceptance of ourselves.

When we meditate, we should not be looking for specific benefits but focus solely on the practice. Only in this way can we train the mind to be focused on the present.

However, the positive effects of this technique are many: when we are aware, we reduce our stress levels, we increase our performance, we know how to evaluate situations with a more critical eye, and we increase our attention to the well-being of others.

Mindfulness meditation gives us moments in which we can suspend judgment and exploit our natural curiosity about the functioning of the mind, approaching our experience with warmth and kindness towards ourselves and others.

Mindfulness, like some of its other "cousins," is a type of meditation that can be performed at any time of the day. It starts with small moments in which you free your mind from its stupor. Over time, it will become easier for you to do this even while performing other actions.

HOW TO PRACTICE MINDFUL MEDITATION

When we talk about meditation, we usually end up having two images: on the one hand, that associated with deep relaxation, detachment from reality, and the feeling of an empty and light mind. On the other hand, the image of a reflection on something, the typical "I'm meditating on what to do," includes the consideration of various aspects of a situation, thoughts on pros and cons, possible consequences, etc.

Mindfulness meditation, or Mindfulness practice, does not correspond to either view. The term mindfulness can be translated into "conscious, accepting and non-judgmental attention."

WHY DOES IT SEEM IMPORTANT TO ACHIEVE INNER WELL-BEING?

Awareness consists in being aware of what is happening to our body, our mind, and the world around us in every moment of existence. In its deepest meaning, it consists in becoming aware of inner emotions and sensations, knowing what these internal experiences are characterized by, what physiological changes they bring about, and what mental states they trigger (how does fear manifest itself? And anger, boredom? What does my body feel in those moments?). Some people are frightened of their inner world and the physical reactions associated with emotions as they do not know them and have never listened to them.

Acceptance

It involves being open to welcoming everything we become aware of, everything we experience, in body and mind. Accepting to feel discomfort, pain, an unpleasant thought. Do not try to drive it away, eliminate it, to stop it. Reacting to the impulse to ease pain (a tingling, an incorrect position, a muscle tension…) leads us to a condition of the motor and mental agitation, to lose the quiet and conscious attention to the present experience. It leads us to follow a quick thought of "I cannot tolerate this discomfort; I have to do something to make it pass," which instead has the potential to increase it. We are paying attention to a thought ("I can't tolerate…" "I have to do…") that is not the reality of the facts (you can tolerate, or at least get to react less impulsively, and you don't have the obligation).

Some do not accept negative feelings for fear that they may harm or cause further suffering, be it physical or mental. Others do this because they have been accustomed to hiding or chasing them away because they have been instructed that it is not a good thing to have unpleasant sensations or have bad thoughts.

The absence of judgment can be seen as an avoidance of brooding on what is happening, why certain thoughts arise, and why we feel a certain way. This allows us not to give judgments and evaluations to the experience we try but to welcome it as a simple event.

During mindfulness practice, we quickly realize how often our mind travels, and we find ourselves far away from conscious attention. Some may be discouraged and consider themselves poorly disciplined pupils. It is important to remember that the goal is to be aware and accepting of all present experiences. You are not a good mindfulness meditator if you have no thoughts or emotions, but rather if you are well aware of what went through your mind and what physical sensations you have experienced, and that you have returned to focus on the present.

BENEFITS OF MINDFUL MEDITATION

At this point, now that you have learned the fundamentals of how to meditate, you may start wondering what the real benefits of meditation are in everyday life. This is a more than legitimate question, and it is perfectly normal to want to see the beneficial effects of the meditative process even in the short term and to want to touch them on the problems we face every day.

At the beginning of your journey, you will immediately find a better control of your thoughts and emotions, as well as a more serene mind and free from unnecessary worries. You will notice this by interfacing with your usual commitments and finding that emotions such as anger, nervousness, and mental confusion will begin to surface in your mind much more rarely until they disappear almost completely. By practicing meditation consistently and perfecting your technique, you can then transfer these benefits to numerous other aspects of your life, from social relationships to your own physical and spiritual health, which can be improved in many ways through specific sessions.

When our mind is aware and present, we have the incredible power to radically change the nature of our days and transform our relationship with ourselves, others, and the world.

Practicing Mindfulness, or Mindfulness, helps us remove the barriers that prevent us from enjoying every moment. Awareness brings us back to the present moment to discover the joy that has always been with us: we were just too busy to notice.

Obviously, meditation is not and will never be an antidote to serious health problems that can only be cured through traditional medicine. However, it represents enormous support and a powerful means of healing for psychosomatic conditions caused primarily by our emotions.

EXERCISES OF MINDFUL MEDITATION

Body Posture

For a full day, try to be constantly aware of your posture. Whether you are sitting, lying, or standing, focus all your attention on your body.

This mindfulness exercise has an immediate effect on restoring our consciousness to the present. The purpose is simply to be aware of the sensations the body is experiencing here and now—

the pressure of the sofa, the ground beneath our feet, or a gentle breeze on our arms.

Learn to simply "scan" your body from top to bottom and notice what sensations are going through it. You just have to do it for a minute or two, then bring your attention back to whatever task you are doing. The goal is to try to observe the posture and the sensations it transmits to you as often as possible during the day.

Meditate on your Breathe

Learning to meditate, focusing only on our breath, and freeing the mind of superfluous thoughts, is the most effective way to cultivate our awareness. Find a quiet place where you won't be disturbed. Sit upright, but don't tense up. Your body should feel relaxed. Soften your gaze and then gently close your eyes, and begin by taking a few deep, cleansing breaths. Allow your mind to become mesmerized by the rhythmic pattern of your breathing.

Many of us do not live in the present moment: we are consumed with memories of the past and worries for the future. But when we meditate and focus all our attention on our breath, we force our mind to the present, as the breath can only exist in the present moment. With constant practice, this simple technique will strengthen our "awareness muscle" to more easily bring Mindfulness into everyday life, even when we are not actively meditating.

Remove the Mental Background

Many of us enjoy listening to music while we work, drive, train or do housework. But without realizing it, it could actually become another distraction to our mind and turn into an obstacle to developing any awareness of the present moment. I always had a soundtrack in my mind, even when I wasn't listening to music—a song inevitably stayed in my head, and I couldn't stop it no matter what I was doing or thinking.

Only when I discovered meditation did I really become aware of the "mental noise" that accompanied me everywhere. My first taste of awareness allowed me to hear this continuous background clearly and realize that I should turn off the radio on my way to work and focus more on my thoughts.

Music could be our way of escaping from reality or finding fun in what is otherwise considered a tedious and mundane activity. But when we are aware of ourselves and practice Mindfulness, inner peace, and stillness correctly that comes from our focus on activity creates a lasting joy that will continue long after the music has stopped.

Indeed, there is no activity that is not worthy of our attention or appreciation - the problem is that we have become accustomed to seeking greater happiness, and we often seek it in the "buzz" that music produces.

Get Rid of the Mental Background!

Next time, rather than filling your head with more noise, try to focus all your attention on the activity itself. Do it as if you were performing it for the first time—be curious. Doing chores or driving, for example, is only boring if you don't pay full attention to the activity.

When driving, don't rush to get to your destination. Even if you're late for work, don't fret - you know you're late, so enjoy the ride! Be aware of the movements of your hands as you shift gears, of your feet as they touch the pedals, and notice the sky and the landscape around you. You can also focus attention on your breath and meditate on it as you drive.

If we truly bring our focus towards the task we are engaged in, then the power developed by our awareness will produce happiness and tranquility that naturally exist in our minds. In this way, your happiness will be stimulated from within, without the need to look for it in external stimuli.

Look, Listen and Feel

Every so often, challenge yourself to find five things that are part of your present experience.

First, notice the top five things your gaze rests on. They don't have to be interesting—it could be a table, cup, rug, or plate in front of you. The goal is simply to bring your full awareness into the present moment. With that done, note five things you can hear. She keeps listening until you have distinguished five different sounds.

Finally, note five things you can feel about your body. It could be the pressure of the sofa, the material of your clothes, a light breeze, tension in your neck, or the air you breathe into your nostrils. There is nothing for you to worry about right now in this present moment. All there is to do at this moment is breathe. Feel your uneasiness slip away with each exhale. Notice how calm you feel as you sit and breathe. Do not think about the breath, but feel it. Feeling the direct sensation of the breath as it comes into the body and leaves the body. Without the need to change it, hold it, or control it. If you notice your mind attempting to shape the breath, or to control it, even in the smallest way, just notice this tendency and allow the breath to flow freely. Noticing the full cycle of the breath. You are not trying to do anything or to get anywhere.

Let your mind wander in this present moment, savor the awareness you just cultivated, and stay immersed in it for as long as you want.

Make your Normal into Sacred

Just because we have to do chores around the house doesn't mean these tasks have to be wearisome and uninteresting. We can transform these activities into mindfulness practices by slowing them down and giving them a different level of attention. Every thought, every action in the light of awareness becomes sacred. In this light, no boundaries exist between the sacred and the profane.

For instance, washing the dishes is both a means and an end. If I am unable to wash the dishes with joy, if I want to finish them quickly to do something else, I will equally be unable to enjoy the next activity with joy. I will think about what to do next, and I will always be carried away by the future, never able to live in the present moment.

These exercises will work toward cleansing your mind as well as allowing you to reign over your mind (in a way that is healthy and in the right proportion because we shouldn't fully always have control over what goes on in our minds).

THE MIND AND BODY CONNECTION

Our health is affected by both bodily and mental factors. It's not one or the other. It is not "mind dominates body" or "mind is irrelevant to the body." Both are equally important.

It is essential to focus on "body" factors such as diet, sleep, and physical activity. But we also have to explore the mind. When we talk about our body-mind connection, you probably imagine someone in a meditative state. However, when we are active, with the blood pumping around our body, we can clearly see how the body and mind work together.

The brain and the body constantly communicate with each other. Your state of mind and mental energy levels affect your mood, so try not to have too much physical or mental stress.

Let's Look at Some Instances

The most common case is the effects of psychological stress on our body: it hinders fat burning, decreases testosterone levels, increases intestinal permeability, and leads to low-grade chronic inflammation, which in turn increases the risk of chronic diseases such as diabetes and cardiovascular disease.

While stress can arise from the mind, we can also lessen physical signs of stress with our thoughts. For example, remembering happy or positive experiences in your life helps you respond better to stressful events, specifically by decreasing the secretion of the stress hormone cortisol.

Imagining doing some exercise or movement activates the same brain patterns that are turned on when you actually do it and even leads to physical improvements. One study found that in healthy, sedentary people, imagining doing biceps curls increased biceps strength by 12-37% without any training.

Practicing meditation physically changes the brain. For example, it increases basal activity in the left side of the prefrontal cortex, a pattern that is associated with positive emotion and reduces the volume of the basolateral right amygdala, changes that are associated with less stress. It also "turns on" genes linked to slowing aging.

Believing that an inert pill will decrease pain (the placebo effect) increases the secretion of opioids and dopamine, which in turn decreases pain. In other words, we have the ability to secrete our own painkillers from our beliefs.

There are a number of things you can do to benefit from the mind-body connection. By reducing stress, you can counteract some of the damaging effects stress has on your body. With mind-body exercises like yoga or tai chi, you can better control anxiety and pain. Some mindful activities can help you renew energy and lift your spirits, and even make you feel more happiness and compassion, thus improving your overall quality of life.

If you're in a state of exhaustion and don't feel like exercising, don't force yourself. Intense exercise is a temporary state of stress for the body that increases cortisol levels and therefore does not help reduce stress. However, exercise improves long-term stress management and will improve your heart and circulatory system. So, in the long run, it will be beneficial.

Listen to your body and your general stress level. If running makes your heart beat faster, it may not be a good idea. You should try a low-impact exercise like yoga. Ask yourself if you feel more relaxed or if you have recovered more. Or if, on the contrary, you still have more stress.

Mind-body connection practices include:

- Gentle movements and meditation, such as yoga.
- Biofeedback is a type of therapy that uses sensors attached to the body to measure key body functions. This therapy

can help you learn more about how your body reacts. In turn, it can help you learn to control your breathing, heart rate, and other functions affected by stress.

- Progressive relaxation is a technique in which one focuses on tensing and then relaxing various muscle groups. This technique can be combined with meditation and breathing exercises to achieve a deep sense of physical and mental relaxation.

To do these practices, you may need to seek help from an experienced guide, mentor, or professional. Though you can do some mind-body exercises in your home, car, or office, and you only need a few moments to do that.

CHAPTER 16

CHAPTER SIX:LETTING GO

Letting go means abandoning what cannot be, allowing us to be freer and more authentic, and preparing ourselves to receive what is to come. Very often, letting go does not mean giving up or forgetting, but simply feeling grateful for what we have lived and consciously turning the page by choosing to keep good experiences, leaving behind us the emotions that do not bring us anything, keep us stuck and make us feel bad.

Letting go or learning not to always keep everything under your grip, to stop insisting on a certain path, situation, relationship, or work just because we believe they are the right one for us and for those around us, is not easy.

Learning, Observing, Letting Go. It's harder to let go of the past when you're not done learning from it. Letting go can bring a sense of freedom and ease. Letting go isn't about overlooking, repressing, or declining everything that's happened to you. Thoughts, emotions, ideas, opinions, beliefs, plans, and sensations are all to be surveyed, inspected, and then let go.

You already know what letting go is. You're always letting go of each breath of air to make room for the next one. To let go of something, you stop holding on to it. The first step is to realize you're holding on to the object in the first place.

What hides the difficulty of letting go?

First of all, the fear of loss and feeling alone leads people to cling in a stubborn and often unconscious way to what has clearly signaled that they no longer want to be held back. In cases where we suffer a loss not necessarily related to a bereavement, the difficulty in letting go is strictly connected to the acceptance of painful feelings, from which we generally tend to defend ourselves. Allowing yourself to fully experience your emotions, even if unwanted, means giving yourself the opportunity to meet and recognize them, thus allowing them the freedom to express themselves in all their fullness.

Another aspect that we struggle to let go of is our ongoing search for safety. We often aspire to ideal situations that we believe can make us feel safe and proud and for which we live in a continuous state of tension, only to discover, once we've reached, how little influential they were on our level of safety and well-being. All this generates a strong sense of frustration.

Finally, one last aspect is the negative conception of change. Change is frightening because it means leaving something certain and known for something unknown when in reality, to grow, to move forward, it is necessary to go through change. No matter how scary it may seem, it will certainly lead to something new, and novelties are good for our minds.

THE STEPS TO LEARNING TO LET GO

How many times have we dared to do something that we felt was right at that moment, such as facing a separation, saying something important in front of a large audience, or letting go of an opportunity, but we were unable to do it?

How many times have you been stubborn about an expectation or a result, such as the outcome of an exam, a job interview, or a dinner with a recently met? We often tense up and keep things from going the way they should.

Use your awareness and willpower, notice the influences you suffer and the limiting beliefs, observe and welcome your fears and follow these seven steps. The results will soon be felt:

1. Observe your Inner Judge

Perhaps others judge you, but you, or rather your inner judge, welcome and takes the judgment into consideration. Just observe what the judge inside you says, how you judge your behavior and work.

2. Welcome

Accept yourself as you would welcome a person with the same difficulty as you and learn to love yourself as you are. Many internal rigidities come from the non-acceptance of ourselves, from the too many demands we have towards ourselves.

3. Remind yourself every day that Anxiety and Expectations keep you from Letting Go

As soon as you hear the voices of anxiety and expectations, find a word to stop them, "stop, silence..." the one you like best and try to distract yourself. Often, they are voices that are not ours but those of those who educated us. We are the masters of our mind, not it of us!

4. Stop and open your mind to the new

If things aren't going your way, stop. Maybe there is something better and more suitable for you waiting for you. Maybe life is trying to make you take a shortcut, and you insist on staying where you are or taking the long way because you are following the reasoning of the head and not those of the heart. If you just stop the following reason and open yourself up to what you don't know, life can surprise you.

5. Let go of Burdens, Memories, and what you no longer need

Memories, thoughts of the past, useless objects. Sometimes it is necessary to get rid of what is no longer needed both in the inner life and in the practical one. Making room is a good exercise in learning to let go.

6. Make room, Slow Down, and Be quiet

They are three fundamental moves to face any moment or choice in life. They are the three moves that guide you to feel what you really want.

7. Take back your power and be aware of yourself

You are the most important voice; life is yours and yours alone. No one else can live it for you, and no one can know what is best and right for you if not yourself!

Trust, let yourself go. Let the seeds you have planted have the right time to sprout... bloom. Leave prejudices and judgments out the door: everything will manifest itself in time and in the right way, in harmony with your soul.

When you let go, you will feel a shift in your energetic field, and a lot of stale energy will be cleared. Letting go will give you space in your heart. What comes and goes is the play of impermanence.

Don't hold on to anything...no desire, no wish. Be totally empty...don't be a container; there's nothing to save, nothing to keep, nothing to remember, nothing to change, nothing to become, and nothing to think about. Don't try to figure anything out.

Letting go of the continual clenching of thoughts, the clenching that resists emotions and makes our mind shrink. When our mind shrinks, we feel miserable, sad, and dispirited. What is the sensation that's associated with happiness? When you see someone you love, someone very close to you, what happens to you? Something in you expands, right? Letting go gives you space. Space brings relief. Space allows expansion. Letting go is liberating.

LETTING GO MEDITATION

Breathing is the practice of letting go. It brings an element of sweetness to our practice: through the breath, we can relax and dissolve tensions.

Concentrate on the breath for a few moments, and see if it helps soften you. Just feel the sensation of the breath going in and out.

Instructions for sitting meditation practice are very simple: you enter your meditation room, set the timer, stabilize your mind as best you can, assume the posture, and gently bring your mind to the breath. I teach my students to start with the breath as a reference meditation object.

There are many reasons why the breath is referred to as a basic meditation object, but a truly excellent one is that it is impermanent. It is always changing. It flows. It is not a stable thing. This means you feel something rather than focusing on something. And at the same time, you cultivate your mind. You train the capacity of the mind to remain present to the impermanence of things: the impermanence of thoughts, the impermanence of emotions, the impermanence of what you see and hear, all things that do not remain stable.

When you sit down, therefore, bring your attention to your breath. Whenever your attention goes off on its own, bring it back to your breath. With the greatest possible precision and clarity, return to the flow of breath, in and out. This doesn't mean keeping an eye on your breath like a hawk—it's not about focusing on your breath. It is to feel the breath, or in other words, being one with the breath. Allow yourself to inhale and exhale. This word, "allow," was once suggested to me by a young woman who I was giving meditation instructions, describing this idea of finding unity with the breath: allowing the breath to come in and out. I found it to very accurately express the feeling of what we do with the breath in meditation because "allowing" conveys a sense of gentleness and non-attachment.

To go even further, you can try to focus your attention on the exhalation and the space that opens at the end of each exhalation before a new inhalation. This focus is like "mixing the breath with space." The breath comes in, and at that point, you can feel a slight pause, a wait, or a void, and then focus your attention on the outside. When the breath goes out, stay as long as you can with that exhalation. Let the breath come out very lightly and relax.

By working with the breath as an object of meditation, you begin to feel that the body and mind come into sync. There is no more division. Meditation can be said to be "the practice of open-mindedness" or "the practice of a natural alert state." Over time, you can ease your focus on the breath and allow yourself to remain still in the open space of the present moment.

To start letting go, we can do some exercise in the meantime. Let's abandon the daily routine for a moment and enjoy the moment (the here and now) just for us. We don't allow anyone to interrupt or distract us.

1. First, we turn off the phone and look for a quiet space where no one can disturb us in the next 10 minutes.
2. Let's sit in a comfortable position with a straight back. The desk chair is fine too.
3. Now, close our eyes and breathe deeply. Each time we exhale, we let go of the weight that we have inside.
4. We listen to the flow of air that enters, invades our body, and slowly exits.

Just watch what emotions come up. Admit the emotions that you're feeling. You don't have to do anything with them. Just be observant of them. Create a distance from your thoughts. If they persist, just continue witnessing them as if from a distance. Don't identify with them. It might help to imagine your emotions and thoughts as bubbles. Like bubbles, understand that these emotions are not solid. They take shape, and they break apart. They are continuously changing shape, blown by the wind.

They come and go. Instead of trying to push the feelings away, allow them to infiltrate through you. Let them dissipate. Let them depart. Now, let the feeling of self-love and peace move into the place you have created.

Ten minutes a day is enough. Who among us would not be able to carve out 10 minutes for ourselves? Have we ever timed how long we spend on social media? You will see how easy it will be to decrease this time and dedicate 10 minutes only to our well-being. There is no right or wrong method to let go.

OBSTACLES TO LETTING GO

The greatest difficulty is not being able to live in the here and now, in the present moment. We are naturally inclined to live in the past, ruminating with anger on past events or living in the future with anxiety for the unknown that awaits us. We can only live in the present by focusing on what we are doing now.

The past has already passed. If things went that way, it means they had to go that way. We stop blaming ourselves for something or feeling melancholy about a certain situation. We're just wasting time. Thinking about something that has already happened, full of guilt, does not make us experience the present and the beauty of what we have around us. We can't change the things of the past, so let's forget about them. What happened has already passed and now ceases to exist.

Likewise, it is useless to be anxious about the future. We do not know what will happen tomorrow, and thinking of a reality that does not yet exist does not help us and makes us more restless. We have to live only in the present moment. We will gradually feel lighter. It is not easy when we have something tormenting us, but we have to try, and the daily practice of listening to our breath will help us.

Another obstacle to failing to let go is our wandering minds. During the breathing practice, the mind brings us worries and does not stay there in the moment. When the mind escapes elsewhere, we try to bring it toward breathing. Let's not get angry. We observe our thoughts by letting them go. Then, let's go back to our own breathing and focus only on the moment.

Another wrong approach to the society we live in is that we do too many things together. At the same time, we are on the phone, we write an email, we notice the shopping list on a piece of paper, and we check the commitments in the afternoon.

We must learn to do one thing at a time with awareness. If we do 10 things together, we don't save time. On the contrary, thinking about ten things at the same time, we will have a loss of concentration during the phone call or in the writing of the email, or we forget some commitment. This loss of concentration creates anxiety, and our performance will certainly be unsatisfactory.

So what to do? Let's try to breathe slowly. The first day will be difficult, the second as well. The third will be a little less hard. After the fourth, we will begin to feel more relieved. The important thing is to start and not postpone. We do not wait for Monday. Let's get started now.

CHAPTER 17

CHAPTER SEVEN:GRATITUDE

Some have described gratitude as just energy, others as a power. That power leads the human being to a deeper connection with the nature of things. The risk is to mistake gratitude for a perennial and forced state of some kind of happiness. Gratitude is not a force to be happy in all circumstances and at any cost, much less an excuse for staying in a negative situation trying to be happy.

In short, being grateful means recognizing and affirming that there are good things in your life and celebrating them. Gratitude gives you the opportunity to improve your life because it leads you to look at the world from a more positive perspective. This means that a mentality aimed at gratitude will never remain in a state of negativity for long. Indeed if we want gratitude, it is an antidote to negativity and helps us to get out of it.

HOW'S GRATITUDE PRACTICED?

Gratitude is a powerful tool unlike any other and is a key to happiness. Practicing gratitude is the easiest key to enhancing your happiness in your daily life. Being in appreciation is a powerful state.

Practicing gratitude means focusing on the most positive and wonderful things we have. Paying attention to what makes us feel good, despite everything. This means giving thanks to life and to ourselves, limiting the bad judgment and criticism that we make every day, and appreciating all the beautiful things surrounding us.

There's always something to be grateful for, regardless of hindrances that are out of our control, and gratitude journals are a simple practice to help keep your blessings on top. No matter how harrowing our current situation may be, there is always a silver lining.

If you always keep longing for things you don't have while hoping they will bring you solace, you will be bitterly disappointed. If you are paying attention and practicing gratitude, you will not hunt after phenomenal moments to seek happiness. It will be right there in ordinary and simple moments. It will enhance your life beyond measure. Most of all, never miss your daily dose of thankfulness.

Journaling, especially gratitude journaling, has proven to have many benefits. It is calming, centering, and downright humbling. Keeping a gratitude journal can gradually provide you with lasting contentment. Also, even in your dark and defeating times, you can find something to be joyful for. So if you feel thankful, write it down. Just take a few minutes out of your day and write three things that you are grateful for.

I personally recommend what I do every night to develop gratitude. Before going to bed, I write in a notebook at least 3 reasons why I am grateful that day; they can be things, circumstances, or people. I write it very specifically.

It is important to make gratitude affirmations. Here's a series of impactful gratitude affirmations.

Take a deep breath and prepare to count your blessings:

- I am grateful for this moment.
- I find something to be grateful for every single day.
- I am thankful for the air I breathe.
- I am grateful for the food that nourishes me.
- I am grateful for a safe and secure home.
- I am grateful for the people in my life.
- I am grateful for where I am today.
- I am thankful for the challenges I have faced.
- I am grateful for the lessons I have learned from them.
- I am grateful for my skills and talents.
- I am grateful for opportunities presenting themselves to me.
- I am thankful for my ability to learn and grow.
- I am grateful for discovering my goal.
- I am grateful for my ability to work towards my goal.
- I am thankful for trusting myself to evolve each day.
- I am thankful for my higher consciousness.
- I am grateful to recognize every blessing, no matter how big or small.

- I am grateful for my sense of gratitude—which brings immense joy and peace to me.

When I check what I have experienced, I reopen the notebooks of gratitude. Our minds are led to remember much more clearly what hurt us. Staring at thoughts of gratitude and remembering good things over time has the power to make people feel more positive and happier.

After writing down the things you are grateful for, read them back to yourself and feel the sense of gratitude inside your heart. 'Feel' them. It's very important to feel them rather than just keeping them in your mind. Be absorbed in gratitude.

SOME BENEFITS OF GRATITUDE

- Grateful people sleep better.
- Gratitude strengthens self-esteem.
- Those who are grateful enjoy better health, both physically and mentally.
- Gratitude increases feelings of joy, optimism, and happiness.
- Gratitude improves the ability to cope with problems and difficulties.
- Reduces stress and toxic emotions resulting from social confrontations, such as envy or resentment (by appreciating the qualities and characteristics of others, we cannot be envious).
- It reduces the sense of regret because we focus more on favorable outcomes.

- Reduces the sense of material attachment. A person devoted to gratitude would be more oriented towards behaviors of generosity.
- Improves social relations, favoring the initiation of new bonds and improving existing ones
- Facilitates the achievement of personal goals.

SAVOR THE LITTLE THINGS OF LIFE

Also, it is important to take time out of your day to savor the little things of life. It encourages self-reflection and is very fulfilling. It makes life worth living. We usually tend to focus on the big things and quantify our lives in milestones. Stop focusing on big events—and start looking for joy in the small moments that happen every day. Take a step back today and appreciate some of the simple pleasures of life. Most people don't at the time. They occur only in hindsight.

Enjoying the little things are important because they comprise the vast majority of our lives. Remarkable events occur sporadically. Small ones happen from moment to moment. When you forsake the little things, you miss out on enjoying a considerable space of your life. The capability to value the small pleasures can upgrade your life in a massive way.

When you take the time to truly relish these tiny moments as they come, you will find that the simple pleasures are what brings great contentment to your life. Simple pleasures are all around you, and you can make use of them anytime. It's not difficult to find them, and there are tons of joys to put on your own list.

To help encourage this joyful habit, I've created a list of simple pleasures for you to celebrate. Savor these to brighten up your day. Here is a list of simple pleasures you should allow yourself to celebrate.

- Taking a deep breath.
- Being present in the moment.
- Waking up after a good uninterrupted sleep.
- The first sip of tea or coffee.
- Aroma of freshly baked bread or cookies straight from the oven.
- The delightful smell of fresh linens.
- The smell of freshly brewed coffee.
- A warm shower after a tiresome day.
- Cold showers on a warm day.
- A daily walk.
- Feeling the sun on your face.
- Experiencing the sensation of a cool and gentle breeze on a warm day.
- Wearing comfy loungewear.
- Reading a book.
- The sound of raindrops.
- Listening to waves.
- The fragrance of aromatic candles.
- Lazy Sundays.
- Watching children play.
- Listening to good music.
- Uncluttered room.
- Chocolate.

- Watching the day's enchanting golden moment - the sunset.
- Sitting in a rocking chair.
- Getting a surprise from your loved ones.
- Doing something nice for someone.
- Seeing people smile.

Everyone's list might slightly differ, but nevertheless, it's these little things that keep us going that can turn an ordinary day into something exceptional.

CHAPTER 18

CONCLUSION

Life is a wonderful experience, and we have a duty to live it with joy and happiness. Then, we go to great lengths to eliminate our sources of stress and anxiety. We accept what has been and that we cannot change, we do not think about the future, and we live in the present, in the here and now. Let's lighten up and smile. I hope you derived joy and liberation from reading this book just like I had written it.